CW01238184

Original title:
The Radiance of Forever

Copyright © 2025 Creative Arts Management OÜ
All rights reserved.

Author: Cassandra Whitaker
ISBN HARDBACK: 978-3-69081-090-6
ISBN PAPERBACK: 978-3-69081-586-4

Shimmering Horizons

In the sky, a sparkle fleet,
Socks that dance on clouds so sweet.
Coffee beans with legs that run,
Jumping jacks, oh what a fun!

Chronicles of the Everlasting

Cats that tell the tales of yore,
Whiskers twitching, they implore.
A time machine made of cheese,
With mice pilots, oh, what a tease!

Prism of Dreams

Rainbows slide down roller coasters,
While penguins wear their cozy posters.
Lollipops that sing and sway,
Jelly beans lead the cabaret!

Unfading Illumination

A lightbulb winks in joyful glee,
Spinning tales of monkey tea.
Chasing shadows who are shy,
Underneath the polka-dot sky.

Light that Never Fades

In a fridge, a bulb burns bright,
Flickering on, then off at night.
It's the light that makes my snacks parade,
A glowing beacon in my lemonade.

Yet sometimes it's a playful game,
With shadows dancing, none the same.
Catch the pickle waltzing in the jar,
That's the glow, my shining star!

The Eternal Flame

A candle's wax drips down with glee,
Pretending it's a waterfall, you see.
It flickers, quirks, and makes me laugh,
As if it's giving me a warm autograph.

Oh, the fire's a picky chef, it seems,
Cooking marshmallows in smoky dreams.
But watch it flicker and try to sing,
For all its sass, it's a warming thing!

A Tapestry of Stars

In the sky, there's a cosmic show,
With twinkling stars that steal the glow.
They're winking down, a cheeky crew,
Playing hide and seek just for you.

One might say they're really shy,
But look closer; they laugh and fly.
Galaxy giggles fill the night,
As I wish on stars, they take flight!

Endless Glimmer

A disco ball spins with flair and fate,
Casting sparkles that dance, oh, wait!
They land like confetti on my nose,
In an epic battle, it's all just prose.

The glimmers giggle, run away fast,
In a gleeful game, they're unsurpassed.
Chasing them brings laughter galore,
As they whisper jokes from the dance floor!

Infinite Horizons

When life gives lemons, make some pie,
Chase the sun while it's in the sky.
Clouds wear silly hats and grin,
Jump on rainbows, let the fun begin!

Wishes fly like kites on strings,
Tiptoe on dreams and see what springs.
Giggling stars in the night parade,
Tickling the moon with a comet's blade.

Luminous Echoes

Whispers dance in the jester's hat,
Winking owls and a playful cat.
Bouncing light, it trips and falls,
Juggling shadows inside the walls.

Waffles sing a syrup tune,
Laughter floats like a balloon.
Echoes of joy in a sugar rush,
Hop on the bus, no time to hush!

Transcendent Moments

Socks that don't match, oh what a sight,
Dancing penguins in a disco light.
Cereal spills with a colorful splash,
Watch the spoon do a belly-flash!

Time tickles, a mischievous tease,
Chasing giggles through the tall trees.
Moments slip like butter on bread,
Who knew laughter could cause such a spread?

Boundless Dawn

Sunshine spills like milk in a bowl,
Silly shadows dance—they have a soul.
Toast pops up with a golden cheer,
Whistling tunes that we love to hear.

Morning fog wears a fuzzy hat,
Peeking around like a shy little brat.
Sleepy yawns turn into bright rays,
Another day where fun always plays.

Celestial Whispers

Stars giggle in the night sky,
Whispers of worlds we can't spy.
Jupiter jokes with a wink,
Mars just twirls, what do you think?

Comets race with candy trails,
Shooting stars tell silly tales.
Galaxies chuckle, spinning 'round,
In cosmic dance, joy is found.

Planets play hide and seek,
Mercury's sass, oh so sleek.
Saturn's rings, a confetti surprise,
Even black holes can crack funny sighs.

So let your laughter take flight,
Across the vast, sparkling night.
With every twinkle, remember this:
The universe loves a droll bliss.

Halo of Dreams

Clouds wear hats, so fluffy and bright,
Dancing around in the soft twilight.
Dreams float by like balloons in the breeze,
Tickling thoughts with mischievous tease.

Napping stars snooze on cosmic beds,
While laughter spills from moonbeam threads.
A comet slips on a cosmic banana,
Leaving behind a sparkly panorama.

Nighttime critters play pranks on the sun,
Chasing the daylight, it's all in good fun.
Jupiter's moons have a stand-up show,
To crack you up, they put on a glow.

So close your eyes, dive into the whim,
Let the giggles of spaceships fill to the brim.
In dreams we'll frolic on joyfully laid schemes,
With a halo of joy, let's tangle in beams.

Unfading Twilight

Twilight giggles as day waves goodbye,
While crickets band together and fly.
Balloons float up, whispering glee,
As shadows play tag with a giddy spree.

Frogs croak jokes from the lily pads,
While owls wear spectacles, looking quite mad.
The moon grins down, a silver coin,
Cows jump over stars with grace, they join.

Fireflies flicker, putting on a show,
With lights and laughter, watch them glow.
They waltz to the rhythm of night's soft tune,
Unfading fun under a whimsical moon.

Let giggles echo in the air so sweet,
In the embrace of twilight, take a seat.
For laughter lingers till morning's ignites,
In the dreamy twilight, where anything bites.

Fragments of Forever

Time has silly socks; they never match,
Day giggles, yearning for a nice scratch.
Nighttime plots with stars in the sky,
Throwing confetti that'll surely fly.

Moments leap like kangaroos in pairs,
Tickling the dawn with playful stares.
Each fragment of laughter extends the fun,
Until time winks and says, 'I'm done!'

Seconds trip over, trying to race,
Willy-nilly in a cosmic chase.
Galaxies toss memories like candy,
Sweet tooth antics, oh so dandy!

So gather the fragments, mix and shake,
In the dance of time, no mistake.
For the joy of now is what we adore,
In the silly space called forevermore.

Glimmering Echoes

In a land where shadows play,
Laughter chases gloom away.
With a wink and a silly dance,
Time rolls by with a goofy prance.

Stars giggle in the night sky,
As moonbeams wink and say goodbye.
A comet trips on its own tail,
And the universe bursts into a laugh trail.

With beams that tickle every chance,
Galaxies spin in a merry stance.
Jokes painted on the cosmic sheet,
Where stardust and chuckles meet.

So let's toast to the endless cheer,
With constellations swaying near.
For in this whimsical delight,
Eternity becomes a comedy night.

A Spectrum of Infinity

Colors clash and dance around,
In a rainbow that won't stay bound.
Sunshine tickles every hue,
While giggles blend in the morning dew.

With each shade that prances by,
Even the clouds chuckle, oh my!
A palette that chortles with glee,
Creating laughter in each spree.

Infinite shades share a joke,
As vibrant tales are often spoke.
The tapestry of humor we weave,
In a spectrum that never leaves.

So let's paint with a playful hand,
And scatter joy across the land.
For laughter in colors will shine,
In this infinity, so divine.

Beacons of the Beyond

Lights flicker like a firefly's wink,
As beyond the stars, we laugh and think.
Each beacon has a story to share,
Of silly moments floating in the air.

Galaxies wave with a friendly toss,
Telling jokes that never get lost.
A black hole might just crack a grin,
As cosmic mischief begins to spin.

Shooting stars zoom in with flair,
Chasing their tails through the cosmic air.
Their twinkling paths like pranks they play,
Bringing giggles to the Milky Way.

So let's dance with the lights up high,
Join the beacons as they fly by.
For in the beyond, smiles ignite,
And laughter echoes through the night.

Boundless Luminosity

Light beams jump and jive around,
In a glow where giggles abound.
Each ray a tickle, every flash,
Like cosmic confetti in a wild dash.

With brightness that refuses to fade,
And shadows in corners trying to trade.
A glowworm in the corner strums,
While laughter erupts from tiny drums.

Crystals sparkle with a cheeky grin,
Reflecting our joy from deep within.
The universe may twist and shout,
As it plays peek-a-boo without a doubt.

So let's bask in this gleeful sight,
Where brightness turns the day to night.
In boundless shades of chuckling light,
We find a reason to unite.

Celestial Emissaries

In the sky, a starfish danced,
Twinkling bright with every glance.
It juggled comets, oh so spry,
While aliens cheered from nearby.

A moonbeam tickled Jupiter's ring,
Promising to teach him how to sing.
But Saturn just laughed, a fidgety twirl,
As a space cat chased a cosmic swirl.

In this galaxy full of glee,
A cactus spaceship sipped its tea.
With laughter bouncing through the void,
Even black holes couldn't be annoyed.

So let's toast to planets that laugh,
And cosmic shenanigans that make us gasp.
For in this universe, wild and bright,
Every tomfoolery shines with delight!

The Luminous Continuum

In a world where socks disappear,
The lost ones dance without a fear.
They twirl around in cosmic play,
Wishing laundry day would go away.

Underwear flies like a rocket ship,
While lint bunnies plot their trip.
They gather dust from every nook,
To write their own best-selling book.

Light bulbs flicker, they can't decide,
To shine bright or to just hide.
They threw a rave one Saturday night,
But forgot the cake, now that's a fright!

In this realm of mismatched socks,
We laugh and dance on ticking clocks.
For who needs sense when joy's amiss?
Each silly moment we can't dismiss.

Serenity in the Starlight

Among the stars, a cat takes flight,
On a quest for fish, just out of sight.
They cast their lines in cosmic streams,
Hooking dreams in twinkling beams.

A dog in a spacesuit leads the way,
Chasing comets, oh what a day!
He barks at moons; they just roll their eyes,
While planets giggle and twirl through the skies.

A cosmic picnic on a cloud so high,
With floating sandwiches, oh me, oh my!
They toast with juice from milky way jugs,
While gravity gives the earth some hugs.

In this dance of cosmic cheer,
Every laugh echoes far and near.
So here's a toast to wild delight,
As stars play tag in the tranquil night.

Flashes of Eternity

In the blink of an eye, toast goes pop,
While jam does a jig, never wants to stop.
With butter in tow, they groove on the bread,
Singing 'We're a team, until we're spread!'

On rainy days, the clouds all sigh,
As raindrops laugh and spin in the sky.
They splash down below, causing quite a stir,
While squirrels in boots show off their fur.

An odd little cactus throws a fit,
Because no one will give him a split.
But in his heart, he knows he's cool,
A prickly king in his desert school!

Thus life marches on, and oh, what fun,
In a world where nonsense is never done.
With giggles and grins, we'll face the day,
For in laughter's embrace, we'll always stay.

Infinite Paths of Light

A penguin in shades slides on the ice,
Claiming he's cooler, oh isn't that nice?
His friends all chuckle, they know he's bold,
But never let him borrow their gold.

A toaster dreams of being a star,
Shooting out toast, both near and far.
But crumbs on the floor are his only fans,
As he grumbles and plans his kitchen bands.

In a park of giraffes, the jokes are tall,
With necks stretched high, they laugh and sprawl.
They dress in ties and debate the weather,
Making their meetings a grand old tether.

So raise a glass to this gala of cheer,
In moments of laughter, we'll always persevere.
With whimsy and joy lighting our way,
Let's dance like no one cares what they say!

Chasing the Horizon

I sprint towards the edge of the day,
Where clouds play tag in a rainbow ballet.
The sun winks like it knows my game,
I stumble and trip, it's all quite the same.

In this race, I slip on a banana peel,
Is that really how I feel, oh what a deal!
The horizon giggles, such a cheeky brat,
As I chase it around, forgetting my hat.

Eternal Flame

I light a match, it flickers with glee,
But burns my fingers—oh why me!
It jumps and dances, like on a stage,
A candle's drama—truly the rage.

My thoughts swipe left on the smoke that swirls,
It whispers secrets, like gossiping girls.
I try to blow it out, but it just has fun,
Chasing my breath, oh who's really won?

Light that Knows No End

A light bulb buzzes, it's quite the hoot,
Glowing so bright in its funky suit.
It flickers in rhythm, a disco ball,
Chasing shadows that run up the wall.

We throw a party, but everyone's shy,
The fridge hums softly, oh me, oh my!
The light decides to do a little dance,
While the toaster burns toast—what a romance!

Spectrum of Time

I wear my watch like a shiny crown,
But minutes run faster, always let down.
Tick-tock, tick-tock, it's all in the race,
Yet somehow I'm stuck, lost in a space.

The calendar laughs, it flips through the years,
While I'm caught between laughter and tears.
Each moment a thread in a colorful skein,
But I keep misplacing my car keys again!

Timeless Fragments

In a world where clocks just laugh,
Time slips by, a silly gaffe.
Tick-tock's gone, it starts to prance,
We dance along, we join the dance.

Cats in hats, and dogs in shoes,
Chasing tails with silly views.
A minute's gone, a jest remains,
Tickling time, we lose our chains.

Laughter echoes through the hall,
What is time? Not worth a call.
Fragments sparkling in the air,
Joyful moments, free from care.

So let's toast to timeless quirks,
In this realm where giggles lurks.
Charming nonsense, we applaud,
Wasting time, our great reward.

Light's Infinite Dance

Silly shadows on the run,
Twisting 'round, they're having fun.
A beam of light that casts a grin,
Shows us where the jesters begin.

Moonbeams giggle, stars in tow,
They waltz along, putting on a show.
Dancing through the neon glow,
Even the sun can't steal the show.

Flashy sparkles, what a sight,
Spinning in the depth of night.
Winks exchanged with every glance,
In this light, we join the dance.

When the sun spills morning glee,
We'll laugh and spin in jubilee.
Forever in this comic trance,
In every twirl, we take a chance.

Celestial Whispers

Among the stars, the jokes are grand,
Like cosmic clowns in a circus band.
They whisper secrets, full of cheer,
Tickling the void, our cosmic sphere.

Pluto pokes at the moon, so bright,
Says, "You're looking clean tonight!"
Jupiter laughs, with rings to show,
A cosmic giggle, not too slow.

Shooting stars zip past with grace,
Winking down at our goofy face.
We catch their tales, a fleeting chance,
In the universe's endless dance.

So here we are, beneath the sky,
Where stardust jokes and comets fly.
In cosmic realms where dreams collide,
We find the laughter that won't hide.

Perpetual Dawn

At dawn we rise, with sleepy grins,
The roosters crowing, just for wins.
Coffee brews, the toast hits high,
Like sunrise giggles in the sky.

Morning light, a playful tease,
Waking up the buzzing bees.
Tickled by the day's embrace,
We start anew at the sun's face.

Sunbeams stretch and giggle wide,
Chasing frost, it's quite a ride.
In haze of morning, jokes are spun,
Forever dawn, and we just run.

So here's to dawn, a joke divine,
Where every moment's dressed in shine.
We laugh, we leap, in endless play,
With every dawn, we greet the day.

Unwritten Destinies

Destinies scribble with glee,
As we tumble through time's spree.
I slipped on a banana peel,
Now I'm dancing, what a deal!

Future's a jigsaw, quite the sight,
A puzzle where cats take flight.
Each mistake sows laughter's seed,
In life's garden, we all proceed.

Past and present play tag,
While I'm stuck in a clever hag.
Wandering paths that twist and bend,
We trip over dreams, my friend.

So here's to fate's funny plot,
With every giggle, a wobbly trot.
Embrace the whimsy, let it rise,
Unwritten tales, oh what a surprise!

Shining Through Time

Tick-tock, the clock does grin,
Time's got a sense of whim within.
I found a watch that runs amok,
Now I'm late and in a schlock!

Moments shimmer like disco balls,
While I trip over glossy walls.
Past me asks, 'Where have you been?'
I reply, 'Chasing my pet squirrel's sin!'

The future chuckles at our plight,
As we stumble into the night.
Laughter glows in every nook,
I just stuck my head in a book!

Secure your hats, it's a wild ride,
With every twist, there's fun to bide.
Shining through the silly veneer,
Here comes time, filled with cheer!

Rays Beyond Existence

In a world lit by quirky rays,
We prance like goats in crazy ways.
Existence throws a party grand,
Where even socks are in demand!

I stumbled on a cosmic joke,
Where trees sing tunes and cats evoke.
Rays of laughter, sparks in flight,
Oh, what a dazzling sight!

Bouncing shadows join the fun,
As we dart beneath the sun.
Existence tickles every bone,
Even rubber chickens have grown!

So let's dance with all our might,
In this realm of joyful light.
With every smile and jolly quirk,
We'll find that beams of fun can lurk!

A Journey of Luminescence

A journey blooms in neon dreams,
Where even doubts are sticky creams.
Glow sticks giggle as we walk,
And silly shadows start to talk.

We sail on boats made of cheese,
Nibbling crumbs that float with ease.
The compass spins, it points to fun,
As we chase a runaway bun!

Adventures shimmer, wild and bright,
With every twist, we take our flight.
Laughter's the map that leads us through,
To lands of joy where dreams renew.

So pack your bags with silly socks,
Join the dance that life unlocks.
On this journey, let's ascend,
In luminescence, my dear friend!

Timeless Illuminations

In a galaxy of socks, where lost colors blend,
Fleeting moments twinkle, like a long-lost friend.
Bouncing here and there, like a rubber ball's flight,
We laugh at the shadows, dancing in the light.

Each grabby hand points, with giggles we burst,
Chasing forever, we quench our cosmic thirst.
Jellybeans orbit, as laughter takes a spin,
In this merry chaos, where do we begin?

Tickles echo softly, through spaceship walls,
A timeless rollercoaster, with its waltzing calls.
Every wink ignites, a star-shaped confetti,
As we trip through the cosmos, so utterly petty.

Oh endless capers, beneath the moon's glow,
Skipping through eons, with nowhere to go.
In our zany universe, with jokes that entwine,
We find sweet eternity in punchlines divine.

Flickers of the Infinite

A toaster pops toast, sending crumbs through the air,
While space squirrels giggle, without a single care.
With each shiny flicker, like stars in a jar,
We toss our worries, while spinning afar.

Banana peels slip, under cosmic delight,
As we dance in the gravity, our limbs take flight.
Floating in laughter, we bounce off the wall,
The universe chuckles, in an echoing hall.

Cotton candy nebulas swirl sweet and bright,
Slurping on stardust, our taste buds ignite.
Twisting through time, we pull silly stunts,
Imitating comets, in brightly colored fronts.

With giggly horizons, where silliness reigns,
We ride laughter waves, through candy-coated trains.
In this whimsical space, where the silly shines clear,
Forever is funnier, when shared with good cheer.

Symbol of Infinity

Wobbly old clocks, tick-tock in a race,
Belly-laughing time, in a haphazard space.
Naps of eternity, with noodles on top,
Each moment's a hiccup, we just cannot stop.

Wormholes are bendy, like my grandma's pet cat,
Who dreams of adventure, on her fuzzy mat.
We juggle realities, while wearing a grin,
With pies flying past, where does chaos begin?

Comets play hopscotch, on cosmic playgrounds,
With blissfully lost stars, painting silly sounds.
Eras turn tumblewheels, as time's silly clown,
In this bubbling whimsy, we twirl upside down.

Infinity chuckles, with playful delight,
As we chase wiggly shadows, into the night.
In the grand cosmic joke, we twiddle and twirl,
Finding joy in the journey, what a wonderful whirl!

Dazzling Threads

Spinning cosmic yarns, of laughter and glee,
We knit quirky galaxies, as bright as can be.
Mismatched socks frolic, in a prancing parade,
While time does the tango, in a dapper charade.

Whispers of stardust tickle our dreams,
In a patchwork quilt of outrageous themes.
Each giggle a fiber, woven tight with grace,
Creating a tapestry of a fun-filled space.

Lollipops twinkle like flickers of hope,
As we surf through the quirks, on a cosmic slope.
The universe teases, with glimmers of light,
In this vibrant patch, everything feels right.

With gleeful regret, we simply let go,
Riding time's merry waves, in a whimsical flow.
In our dazzling adventure, where laughter is threaded,
We find joy in the journey, cozily embedded.

The Glow of Timelessness

In a world where clocks just laugh,
The seconds dance upon the path.
With giggles of the timeless clocks,
We wear our socks like silly rocks.

Time's gone wild, it lost its game,
Each minute teases, what a shame.
With every tick, my hat goes up,
And jelly beans fill every cup.

The past is now a prankster's jest,
With jokes and gags, it feels the best.
We skip along on puddles bright,
As laughter lights the endless night.

So here's to days without a care,
When every moment's like a fair.
With joy that plays in endless rounds,
And humor that forever bounds.

Dancing Flames of Today

In the oven, cookies tease,
They dance and spin just like the breeze.
A marshmallow doing the cha-cha,
While popcorn pops a silly raga.

Sparklers shine with all their might,
Like fireflies in a frolicking flight.
They tickle flames with giddy glee,
As hot dogs waltz on skewers, whee!

Bananas slip with style and grace,
In this wild, zany kitchen space.
While toast performs a little jig,
I roll my eyes, then start to gig.

So fry it up, and let it sway,
In this buffet of the buffet.
We'll feast and laugh the night away,
In kitchens where the flames will play.

Boundless Skies

The clouds are cows, just floating high,
They moo and drift, oh my, oh my!
With wings of cheese and giant pies,
They paint the blue with fun surprise.

Kites that giggle, swoop and dive,
In winds that cheer, they come alive.
Like choir boys, they sing a tune,
With tail as bright as a full moon.

Little birds wear tiny hats,
While squirrels plan their acrobat chats.
The stars drop sparkles down in cheer,
As constellations grin from here.

So lift your eyes and have a laugh,
At fleeting clouds that dance and quaff.
In boundless skies with joy to share,
Every giggle floats up in the air.

Unveiling the Infinite

An endless scroll of silly memes,
With kittens riding on swift beams.
A puppy's face, a loaf of bread,
In timeless loops of giggly thread.

Peeking through the curtain's seam,
A never-ending fun-filled dream.
With jokes that fly and pranks that laugh,
Computers powered by our gaff.

Infinity wears comical shoes,
While time just fumbles with its clues.
Riddles float in space's chest,
Tickling hearts with playful jest.

So join the dance of endless mirth,
As laughter echoes through the Earth.
In realms where joy's the only key,
Unveiling tricks for you and me.

Glowing Moments

In a world of glow and gleam,
Where even puns can brightly beam,
I tripped over my own two feet,
And laughed so hard, I spilled my treats.

Chasing shadows, silly thoughts,
Each twist and turn, my mind forgot,
I blundered into a tree so stout,
It whispered secrets, made me shout.

Light bulbs blink with mischief bright,
Jokes take flight in the starry night,
A comet sings a funny tune,
As laughter dances 'round the moon.

So let's embrace this gleeful phase,
With silly games and sunny days,
For every moment that we shed,
Is brightened up with joy instead.

Veil of Perpetuity

Behind the curtain, a light does twink,
A smirk from fate, what do you think?
The cat dressed up in fancy wear,
Took charge and waltzed without a care.

I stumbled on a glowing snail,
That told me jokes; oh, how we'd wail,
It slimed a path across the floor,
Each laugh it shared, I asked for more.

The moon wore shades, a stylish trait,
While stars arranged a silly date,
A cosmic clown with vibrant hue,
Danced through the night, just me and you.

So as we peek behind the veil,
In giggles, let our hearts set sail,
For every grin and happy sigh,
Transcends the limits of the sky.

Echoes of Luminous Days

With echoes bouncing off the walls,
I chased a ghost; it took great falls,
In silver shoes, it danced away,
Tickling us both without delay.

The sun wore shades, a funny sight,
And napped 'til noon, what pure delight,
It tossed a wink, a wink we stole,
And filled our hearts, we couldn't bowl.

In radiant rumbles, laughter roars,
As kittens plot their little wars,
Each gleeful meow, a bright parade,
In silly antics, friendships made.

So let's embrace these glowing rays,
With laughter echoing through the days,
Find joy in every little sprout,
And in the silliness, we'll shout.

Continuum of Brightness

In flashes bright, ideas zoom,
A dancing light bulb shakes the gloom,
It tells a joke that makes us cheer,
As laughter bubbles into the sphere.

With sparklers twirling, oh so grand,
We twirled around, hand in hand,
Each joke a spark, we joined the spree,
In a cyclone of glee, just you and me.

A rainbow chases down the lane,
With painted hooves, all drenched in rain,
It stopped to giggle, made it rain,
With colors bright, it eased our pain.

So let us frolic in this space,
Where brightness meets a smiling face,
In every joke, let's find the flair,
And dance with joy, beyond compare.

The Light that Time Forgot

In a dusty old attic, the bulbs gather dust,
They flicker their jokes, in shadows they trust.
A chandelier giggles, swaying with flair,
While a lamp starts to dance, without any care.

Old clocks tick and tock with a snickersome tone,
They wager on time, like kings on a throne.
While a pesky sunbeam slips under the mat,
Whispering secrets, "You're late! How about that?"

An ancient device for a hairdryer's heat,
Overheats and sneezes, "I need a cold sheet!"
In this realm of nostalgia, all laughter's a must,
For even the light knows it's time that won't rust.

So cherish the goofs of forgotten delight,
As giggles of light sprinkle the night.
In laughter we bask, with time by our side,
As shadows and bulbs take us for a ride.

Enduring Silhouettes

Beneath a grand moon, the silhouettes prance,
A couple of trees do a blossomy dance.
With branches that sway, they throw shade and cheer,
Stealing the spotlight without any fear.

A cat on a fence, with an air of pure pride,
Claims the whole garden, it's their special ride.
While the wind has a chuckle, sneezing with grace,
Giving the hedges a ticklish embrace.

An owl in the moonlight does laugh from afar,
With its wise little eyes, an eternal superstar.
It hoots out old jokes about squirrels in suits,
As shadows all snicker, swapping their roots.

In shadows and light, the comedy flows,
With every odd angle, a new humor grows.
So dance with the silhouettes, let laughter ignite,
For life's just a sketch bathed in whimsical light.

Illuminated Horizons

A sun that sleeps late causes quite the fuss,
While dawns throw their tantrums—just a silly plus.
Colors in puddles play hopscotch at dawn,
As the sky paints a tale with each giggling yawn.

Clouds wear their fluff, in a poofy parade,
With rainbows that wink, teasing us in spades.
Laughter erupts, as they tumble and race,
Chasing horizons, they keep up the pace.

Amidst all the fun, are birds on a spree,
Singing off-key is their melody.
With a wink and a flap, they mock what they hear,
While the blushing sun grins ear to ear.

So raise up the cheers, let the colors collide,
For humor is bright in this whimsical ride.
Illuminated moments tickle the night,
In the dawn's giggle, we find pure delight.

Paths of Infinite Light

On paths where the glowbugs swarm and they tease,
Frisky little critters dance over the breeze.
They blink out their jokes in a flicker and flash,
While shadows conspire in a soft, silent clash.

Dandelions giggle, they scatter their fluff,
Saying, "Catch us if you can, it's not really tough!"
As pathways of laughter wind near and afar,
With a wink and a nudge, like a comedic car.

Starlight rumbles softly like thunder from cheer,
While the night wears a crown, "Let's spread joy, my dear."
Every footstep's a punchline in trails of delight,
As lanterns of wonder illuminate the night.

So wander the pathways where giggles reside,
For light's just a lark when you're along for the ride.
With every soft beam, let your spirit take flight,
On paths filled with joy, in the embrace of the light.

Celestial Reflections

In the sky where stars play hopscotch,
The moon sings while comets botch.
Angels giggle in a cosmic dance,
While planets argue, 'Who wears the pants?'

Galaxies twirl like they've had a drink,
Gravity's joke makes us stop and think.
Jupiter's snacks are quite a delight,
While Saturn's rings sparkle, oh what a sight!

Nebulas puff like cotton candy,
Asteroids zoom, but are never dandy.
Black holes suck in all the fun,
But they still can't catch a wayward pun!

So next time you gaze at the skies so bright,
Remember the laughter that travels all night.
The universe chuckles in infinite jest,
Leaving behind its sparkly rest.

Ageless Brilliance

Time ticks in a cosmic clock tower,
Yet leaves us with a silly flower.
The sun coughs, spilling sunshine rays,
While old stars share their youthful days.

Wrinkles of space, textures of time,
Planets stumble in a rhythm and rhyme.
Old meteors tell tales with a twist,
Of black holes that simply can't desist!

Quasars roar with a mighty cheer,
While light years play hide and seek near.
Galactic giggles echo out loud,
As the universe wears its most amusing shroud.

Adventures unfold with a splash and a tease,
As comets tickle the cosmic breeze.
In a realm where humor never ends,
The age of the stars creates vibrant trends.

Nocturnal Radiance

At night the stars throw a wild bash,
While owls hoot, making quite a splash.
Fireflies flash like disco lights,
And shadows dance with a wink of delights.

Moonlit mischief fills up the sky,
As nighttime critters wink and fly.
Raccoons tiptoe in search of a snack,
Stealing stars, but they always come back!

Clouds gather like a chattering crew,
As the night wears its shimmering hue.
Shooting stars compete in a race,
But trip over laughter in outer space.

The cosmos chuckles beneath its veil,
While unicorns prance on a shooting rail.
Let's dance beneath the stars till dawn,
Where every giggle is reborn!

Boundless Glow

In a realm of light that never fades,
The sun cracks jokes as daylight parades.
With every beam, it delivers a laugh,
While shadows blush in confused aftermath.

Rainbows prance with colors so bright,
Tickling clouds in a feathery flight.
Butterflies flutter with giggling grace,
While the sun says, 'Catch me if you can,' in a race!

Balloons of stardust float up high,
As planets spin in a cosmic pie.
Laughter echoes from each shining place,
As every twinkle wears a playful face.

So come join in this gleeful show,
Where joy and chuckles endlessly flow.
In the glow that knows no end,
Each grin and laugh, our best friend!

Beams of Unending Time

A clock once told a silly joke,
It tickled me until I broke.
I laughed so hard, I lost my place,
And now I can't find time or space.

The sun wore shades, a cool teen vibe,
While moonbeams danced, a jolly tribe.
Stars giggled through their twinkling eyes,
As comets raced, yelling, "Surprise!"

The past tried hard to tell a tale,
But tripped on words, and started to bail.
Yet memories shine, with a wink and a grin,
Like candy wrappers tossed in the wind.

Future floated in on a bright balloon,
Singing off-key to a silly tune.
Time's a circus, with no end in sight,
Under a tent made of pure starlight.

A Tapestry of Light

A glow worm wore a fancy dress,
Claiming to be the light's success.
But glow bugs laughed, saying, "Not quite!"
They shone together, a silly sight.

A rainbow spilled, like a colorful mess,
With paint cans flung, in sheer excess.
Each color fought, for the best position,
Creating chaos, a bright rendition.

In the sky, the sun spilled tea,
On clouds that giggled, filled with glee.
"It's time for fun!" the stars all cheered,
As laughter echoed, brightly smeared.

The moon told jokes, with a cheesy grin,
But the stars just rolled, they could not win.
Together they spun, in a playful race,
Creating a tapestry, time can't erase.

The Whispering Cosmos

Among the stars, the cosmos sighs,
Sharing secrets, in comical ties.
Galaxies giggle, spinning round,
As planets bump, in a boisterous sound.

Neptune's joke was not too clean,
It made the rings burst out in sheen.
Uranus turned, with an awkward face,
Claiming some gas, just out of place.

Saturn laughed, as it swayed and twirled,
With its shiny rings, it danced and whirled.
A supernova popped, like a big surprise,
While black holes whispered, "Is this a guise?"

Time wears sneakers, racing through space,
Chuckling and hiccuping, in a silly race.
The universe giggles, its story unfurled,
With each twinkling wink, a joke is hurled.

Trails of Luminous Echoes

Once a photon tried to stroll,
Tripped on gravity, lost control.
It zipped and zapped, left quite a trace,
Of sparkles and giggles, all over the place.

A comet decided to play hide and seek,
But the stars protested, "That's just bleak!"
So they joined forces, in a grand game,
Launching light trails, chasing the fame.

The universe hums a playful tune,
With nebulae dancing, under the moon.
Light bursts forth, with a wink and a glare,
As echoes giggle, filling the air.

Time draws a doodle, with crayons of light,
Creating a canvas, brilliant and bright.
In this comic ballet, everything flows,
As the laughter of cosmos endlessly grows.

Shimmering Eternity

A light bulb in heaven thinks it's a star,
But flickers and sputters, it's just bizarre.
It bends light like crazy, throws shadows around,
While angels all giggle as they dance on the ground.

A comet's a taxi, zooming through space,
Pick up a stardust, let's liven the place!
But each time it lands, it just goes on strike,
Guess celestial travel just isn't their type.

The Moon took a selfie; it's a little unclear,
With craters and shadows, it looks full of… cheer!
While Earth looks on, trying hard not to crack,
Saying, "What's with that filter? Just take it all back!"

So here in this cosmos, we laugh all night long,
With stars as our lanterns, we sing silly songs.
A universe of jesters in costumes so bright,
A shimmering eternity—a comic delight!

Everlasting Illumination

A sunbeam thought dancing would be quite the glee,
But tripped on a cloud and fell right into tea.
The wind blew a chuckle, as raindrops all twirled,
An everlasting laugh in this wacky world.

Light bulbs debate if they should wear shades,
While fireflies giggle, and the light parade fades.
'We're the brightest!' they claim, but oh what a sight,
With bugs wearing goggles, it's a glorious night!

A glowworm named Larry snagged a date with the Moon,

But gossiped to stars about how to swoon.
"Just sparkle and twinkle!" they'd all shout with glee,
While Larry just blinked, "But that's not really me!"

So laughter and light intermingle with grace,
In everlasting illumination—the quirks we embrace.
Each twinkle's a joke, like a secretive wink,
In the cosmos, we find that we all love to sync.

Glimmers of Infinity

In the sofas of space, where all the stars lounge,
They binge-watch black holes and giggle at sound.
The comets on cushions, with popcorn in hand,
Glimmers of infinity, the best night so planned.

A galaxy's DJ spins records of time,
While planets groove sideways in a twisted rhyme.
The asteroids rock out, but get lost in the beat,
Hurling past Mars, where they think they're so neat.

The Moon throws a party, but forgot all the snacks,
They offered some craters, just crumbled like hacks.
As Saturn's rings sparkle, they whisper, "Oh dear!"
"Is that all you brought? It's a cosmic career!"

In these glimmers of joy, we twirl and we swirl,
With planets and stars that all giggle and twirl.
Infinity's laughter, it echoes and sings,
In the vastness of space, we've the silliest things.

Ageless Reflections

In a pond of starlight, frogs sing out loud,
Reflecting on ages in a cosmic crowd.
They croak about time like it's one big prank,
While splashing on ripples, a shimmer-y tank.

The sun's always shining, with a grin on its face,
"Just look at my rays! I'm the king of this place!"
But planets just chuckle, "Oh Sun, take a break!
Your light's great and all, but don't overthink."

A wise old tree whispers tales of the sky,
"Time's just a circle with a pizza pie."
With stars as the toppings, they laugh in a ring,
Ageless reflections, oh the joy that they bring!

So gather round closely, let the laughter grow,
With echoes of time as our vibrant show.
We'll dance with the comets, we'll sing with the breeze,
In an ageless embrace, it's the best kind of tease!

Celestial Portals

In the sky, a portal glows bright,
Aliens juggling and setting their sights.
Far from Earth on a wild pizza spree,
They forgot their spaceship, oh, woe is me!

A comet rushes by, a blink of an eye,
Where did it go? Oh, there it flies high!
Chasing moonbeams like kids on a quest,
With tinfoil hats, they think they're the best!

Stars are winking with glimmers of glee,
Making faces at planets like, 'Look at me!'
Elves at the helm, steering far and wide,
Was it a joke? Or a cosmic slide?

Galactic hiccups, what a sight to behold,
Shooting stars trading tales that are bold.
In this fun dance of the improbable feast,
Who knew the universe had such a tease?

Shining Threads of Time

Time twinkles like a rogue little sprite,
Knitting moments with threads oh-so-bright.
Every stitch a laugh, every loop a cheer,
Stuck in a sweater? Oh dear, oh dear!

Grandma's tales woven through history's loom,
In plaid and polka dots, she enters the room.
While mischievous clocks tick-tock and they prank,
Unraveling yarn that smells like a tank!

Puppies and kittens crawl into the yarn,
Ripping the fabric with innocent charm.
Tickling our noses whilst running around,
As our time machine spins with giggles profound!

The past and the future in knots, all in fun,
Slide down the threads like a race just begun.
In this weaving of joy, we find that we chime,
A tapestry full of giggles through time!

Luminous Footprints

Footprints in light, oh, what a scene,
Echoes of laughter where darkness has been.
Dancing around in shoes not our size,
Tripping and tumbling, what a grand prize!

Each sparkling step leaves a giggle behind,
As shadows and whimsy together entwined.
Who wore those clown shoes? What a ruckus made,
Is that our own laughter or a joke well-played?

Moonlight's a prankster that tickles the ground,
With whispers of wonders in giggles abound.
We chase with delight, these glows and these baits,
Giving high-fives to our silly fate!

The path is a laughter, it stretches so wide,
With luminous footprints, we take in our stride.
In jest with the universe, we dance and we sway,
Under the twinkling, light-hearted array!

Unbroken Illumination

A light that won't flicker, won't fade away,
Cracked jokes like a lamp that just loves to play.
With a wink from the bulb like, 'What do you mean?'
Illuminating laughter where gloom has been seen!

Flipping the switch, oh, what a delight,
A comedy show under the glow of the night.
Butterflies laugh, and the shadows take flight,
For every chuckle, the darkness takes fright!

Funny how beams can twist and can turn,
Lighting up corners where shadows discern.
With bulbs in the audience, laughter's the aim,
And each giggle's a spark, igniting the flame!

So here's to the moments, so bright and so clear,
When humor shines through, and we shed every fear.
For in this great theatre of comedy grand,
Unbroken giggles, hand in hand, we stand!

A Tapestry of Glows

In a land where socks go to hide,
Bright beacons whisper, never to chide.
Dance with the giggles that twinkle and spin,
A parade of light where troubles wear thin.

Jellybeans glow, and the gumdrops sing,
Luminous laughter, oh, what joy they bring.
Bubblegum clouds float on marshmallow skies,
As silly as jelly, where no one denies.

Chuckling stars peek through the night,
Tickling the moonbeam with cheeky delight.
Each twinkle a wink, a giggle, a cheer,
A glowing adventure, come join us, my dear.

Frolicking fireflies ride on the breeze,
Wobbling wonders, they dance with such ease.
With each flicker and blink, they share their cheer,
In this vibrant realm, all worries disappear.

Crystalline Dreams

In the land where dreams take a dive,
Jellyfish sparkle, making fun thrive.
A disco ball spun by a sleepy cat,
Frogs sporting berets, imagine that!

Lollipops twirl on the candy cane street,
Sippin' on sunshine, a delightful treat.
The cupcakes giggle, their frosting so bright,
In this glassy wonder, everything's light.

Diamonds in laughter, gleaming so wide,
Even the shadows come out for a ride.
Hopskipping fairies with twinkling feet,
In a world of gems, life can't be beat.

Clocks that chuckle go tick-tock in style,
Each moment a dance, stretching a smile.
So come spin with us, it's an odd little scheme,
In these crystalline moments, we live out our dreams.

Eternal Glow

A pickle parade on a neon sea,
Dancing with veggies, what joy to see!
Olive oil lamps hum a silly tune,
Under the watch of a giggling moon.

Bananas in bowties, a classy flair,
Twirling their peels like they don't have a care.
Each chuckle a spark, lighting up the night,
In this wild banquet, everything's bright.

Dandelion wishes float up on high,
Riding a breeze, making time fly.
In the realm of the goofy where laughter's the key,
We bask in the glow of our sweet jubilee.

Outrageous moments where shenanigans bloom,
Catch the warmth of the glow, let joy fill the room.
For in every tickle and silly little show,
Life's a brilliant canvas, with an eternal glow.

Luminescent Journeys

Off we go on a train made of cheese,
Chugging along with such delightful ease.
Moonlight waffles on our plates they lay,
As we giggle our way through a bright buffet.

In quirky towns where umbrellas float,
Pandas ride bicycles, making us gloat.
Jumping in puddles of sparkling cheer,
Each raindrop is friendly, come join us, my dear.

Glow-in-the-dark jellybeans race by,
As we traverse tunnels beneath the sky.
With each loop and swirl, we break into laughter,
On this odyssey, joy is the master.

So buckle up tight; let's have some fun,
In this silly escapade, we're never done.
With every delight, stars shine and beam,
In luminous journeys, we're living the dream.

Shadows of Forever

In a land where shadows play,
The moon's lost its way.
Chasing its tail in the night,
It thinks it can take flight.

Wandering far, a clumsy sight,
Bumping trees with all its might.
A raccoon laughs, can't hold its glee,
"Hey moon, you ain't as smart as me!"

Stars giggle, covering their eyes,
As the moon trips, oh what a surprise!
"Next time, I'll stick to my groove,"
But no one believes his next move.

So as shadows dance on the ground,
The moon's confusion is tightly wound.
Forever chasing, always a mess,
A shadowy tale of silliness!

Glints of Timelessness

In a world where clocks freeze at noon,
Time's lost the Beat, thinks it's a tune.
Tick-tock is just a faint cheer,
As everyone's nose grows long, oh dear!

The past throws a party, it's wild!
Future shows up, just a lost child.
"Hey, can I borrow a minute or two?"
"Sure, but you owe me a trip to the zoo!"

Now present, quite grumpy, turns bright,
Trying tricks to make time feel right.
With jokes and pranks, it dances around,
Rejoicing in chaos, what a sound!

Laughter echoes, oh what a sight,
Even seconds have joined in the flight.
Time's shenanigans are plain to see,
In glints of fun, forever free!

The Luminous Odyssey

In a ship made of dreams and giggles,
Sailing through stars and their wiggles.
A captain who wears a hat of cheese,
Steering the ship with bashful ease.

Pirates of laughs, they joke and tease,
"Let's pillage some chocolate, if you please!"
Through cosmic seas they boundlessly roam,
Finding treasure maps made of foam.

A comet zooms by, what a sight!
"Is that a candy?" they shout with delight.
But alas, it's just a star that's gone shy,
Leaving the crew to laugh and fly high.

With taffy clouds and jellybean skies,
Keep giggling, the universe tries.
In their luminous journey, they blend,
Wearing laughter like a timeless trend!

Celestial Treasures

Stars hold secrets in their glows,
Like a cosmic game of peek-a-boos.
While comets giggle and shoot on by,
Hiding treasures in the sparkle of the sky.

A star cluster laughs, "Catch me if you dare!"
As planets chase it without a care.
"Bet I can twinkle brighter with style!"
"Oh please, you just make us laugh for a while!"

A black hole winks, "I'm on a diet!"
While asteroids whisper, "Try it, why fight it?"
In the dance of the cosmos, what a show,
Where fun and chaos paint the glow!

So if you gaze at the sky tonight,
Remember the giggles, the sheer delight.
Amidst the wonders, forever they gleam,
In celestial treasures, join the dream!

Polished Memories of Light

In a world where time takes a leap,
Lamps come alive, secrets to keep.
They giggle and shimmer, dance on the floor,
Each glow a tale, begging for more.

Shadows whisper, glitter's delight,
A disco ball shines, oh what a sight!
Memories twirl in a sparkly spin,
Who knew glimmers could let us in?

Sock puppets join in on the fun,
Under the glow of a bright fuzzy sun.
Laughter like bubbles floats in the air,
Each flicker of joy, an electrifying flare.

So let's toast to the glow and the gleam,
In this wacky, wild, whimsical dream.
With light as our guide, we'll tiptoe along,
In polished memories where we all belong.

Celestial Refrain

Stars are winking in a heavenly jest,
Comets laughing, they're feeling the best.
Jupiter's got jokes, so quirky and bold,
While Pluto rolls eyes, just doing what's told.

Galaxies twirl in a dizzying race,
Each supernova puts on a funny face.
The Milky Way giggles and swirls around,
While black holes burp, no silence found!

Asteroids skipping, a cosmic ballet,
Orbiting planets join in the play.
With stardust giggles, they dance in delight,
Celestial beings, what a hoot, what a sight!

And as we look up at this glittering spree,
We laugh at the chaos of all that we see.
In this universe, joy takes its place,
In a celestial refrain, we're embraced by grace.

Illuminating Eternity

A lantern hangs, sways in the breeze,
Telling tales of pirates with embarrassing sneeze.
They plundered the seas, but not without fear,
Of acaptain who hiccupped whenever he neared!

Time keeps ticking in its quirky way,
With clocks playing pranks, oh what a display!
Each tick a giggle, each tock a jest,
Tickled by moments that never find rest.

Suns chuckle, moons wink, in the great night sky,
While planets parade, with a laugh and a sigh.
Eternity glimmers in this playful dance,
A comedic routine, an extraordinary chance.

So let every sparkle bring a smile wide,
In illuminating tales that we ride.
With humor alight in our hearts and our minds,
We chase after shadows, leaving laughter behind.

Resplendent Narratives

In the library of light, tales come alive,
Books whisper giggles, as they take a dive.
A story of cats who cook with delight,
Who prepared a feast, served up with a fright!

Pages flutter, sharing puns galore,
With lines that tickle, we ask for more.
Adventures unfold with a twist and a grin,
As words leap and prance, inviting us in.

Words dance like fireflies, brightening the dark,
With characters silly, each leaving a mark.
The saga spins on, with laughter its king,
In resplendent narratives, joy's the main thing.

So let's read together, by the flickering flame,
In the library of life, we'll never be the same.
With humor encapsulated in each joyful line,
We'll enjoy the stories, forever entwined.

Whispers of the Celestial

When stars play hide and seek at night,
They giggle, twinkle, oh what a sight!
The moon tells jokes that are quite absurd,
Even the comets aren't shy, haven't you heard?

Galaxies swirl in a cosmic dance,
Tripping over space-time, what a mischance!
Planets chuckle, orbit in glee,
With each silly wobble, they shout, "Look at me!"

Asteroids crash with a playful clang,
Rockets zoom by with a boisterous clang!
While black holes yawn, sucking up fun,
"In the void, I'll nap; I've barely begun!"

And when the sun rises, the laughter subsides,
But whispers of stardust forever abide.
In the cosmic playground, joy is the rule,
Join the starlit party, it's all very cool!

Forever Aglow

A light bulb's glow in the fridge at night,
Is an epic showdown, a comical sight.
While veggies rattle with gossip inside,
"Why are we here?" they giggle and hide!

The candles flicker with mischievous flair,
In their soft dance, they spin without care.
"A waxy waltz!" they whisper with glee,
"Let's light up the world, just you and me!"

The sun in the morning wears shades with a grin,
As if it knows where the fun will begin.
"It's a bright day!" it shouts with delight,
"Let's dazzle the clouds and give them a fright!"

So let's bask in laughter, let joy be our flow,
With sparkles of humor continuing to grow.
In a universe filled with wondrous light,
We'll chuckle and frolic through day and through night!

Harvesting Starlight

In a field of dreams, we plant tiny beams,
With rakes made of laughter, we gather our dreams.
"Here comes a comet!" a farmer will shout,
"Quick, catch its tail before it zooms out!"

Sowing seeds of chuckles, we watch them all sprout,
While moonbeams giggle, swirling about.
"Oh, see that shooting star?" a child grins wide,
"Quick, wish for snacks, let's have a joyride!"

With galaxies wrapped in twinkling delight,
We forage for giggles that shimmer so bright.
"Let's dance with the fireflies!" one owl declared,
And so they all twirled, with fun they fared!

Our harvest is laughter, our bounty pure cheer,
With whims of the cosmos, there's nothing to fear.
In the garden of wonders, we all have a part,
As starlight tickles the giggles of heart!

Invincible Spark

A spark ignites with a pop and a fizz,
It tickles our senses, what a dazzling whiz!
In the realm of silly, it dances with flair,
Brightening spaces like a breath of fresh air.

With winks and jumps, it twirls on its head,
"Catch me if you can!" it giggles and sped.
It tickles the feathers of every small bird,
Making them laugh, while they flop and they stirred!

In the glow of the twilight, it winks at the moons,
"Let's throw a party, with silly cartoons!"
A jester of brightness, it jives with delight,
Inviting the cosmos to join in the night!

So hold close the joy, let it light up your day,
With sparkles of humor to brighten the way.
Together we'll sparkle, with giggles that hark,
In this grand universe, we'll dance like a spark!

Eternal Light

In the fridge, the glow does shine,
Leftovers dance, they seem divine.
A light so bright, it steals the show,
Must be the jelly, or maybe Joe.

Lampshades chuckle, lampshades prance,
Daytime slumber, light takes a chance.
Tripping on wires, I make my stand,
Lighting my way with a pizza brand.

Candles wink with a friendly fizz,
Chasing shadows, what a whiz!
In every corner, a party waits,
Just don't invite those pesky plates.

Glow worms giggle in nighttime glee,
Singing tunes of "Watch out for me!"
They twirl and spin, what a delight,
Unruly bugs, the stars in flight.

Whispering Stars

Stars chuckle softly in the sky,
Telling secrets on the fly.
"Hey, did you hear about the moon?"
"Yeah, it's a real late-night cartoon!"

Planets jitterbug, dancing bold,
Spinning tales that never get old.
Falling comets, in joyful zest,
"Catch me if you can!" they jest!

Nebulas giggle and swirl about,
Creating shapes, there's never doubt.
"Is that a cat? Or just my hair?"
"Who cares? Let's blow space without a care!"

Galaxies wheeze, they laugh and spin,
Pluto sings, "Let's jump right in!"
Together they dance, no need to rest,
Out in the void, they're truly blessed.

Timeless Glow

A glowing clock makes quite a scene,
Ticking tunes like a seasoned machine.
"Time flies!" it says with a smirk,
"Join the fun or face the quirk!"

Old photographs twinkle with glee,
Dancing memories, come join me!
"Remember this? The socks and the shoes?"
Laughter abounds, we can't lose!

Calendars giggle, flipping the page,
"Next month's party? Bring your sage!"
With paper hats and plenty of cheer,
"It's time to celebrate, let's all draw near!"

Yesterday's jokes, in a timeless flow,
Relive the moments, they steal the show.
The sun keeps shining, fun never ends,
In this whimsical realm, laughter extends.

Celestial Embrace

Sunbeams high-five, a cheerful view,
Clouds giggle, "Nothing else will do!"
With every ray, a wink and grin,
Let's dance along; let the fun begin!

Rain drops splatter, making art,
Puddles reflect wit, playing their part.
"Jump in and splash!" shouts a young grin,
Nature's laughter is where we begin.

Wind whispers tales of playful glee,
Tickling branches, ruffling me.
"In every breeze, joy's to be found,
C'mon, let's spin 'round and round!"

As stars unwind in the night's embrace,
They cheer on the moon, "Set the pace!"
With each twinkle, a joke takes flight,
In this cosmic prank, we find our light.

www.ingramcontent.com/pod-product-compliance
Ingram Content Group UK Ltd.
Pitfield, Milton Keynes, MK11 3LW, UK
UKHW022105050225
454743UK00006B/86